SARASWATI

Mitali Sengupta

SARASWATI

Once upon a time, Lord Brahma, seated on a beautiful, pink lotus, decided to create this world. However, His creations were all going topsy-turvy! Brahma was upset and did not know what to do. He was all alone and needed somebody to help him with his creations. 'Oh, I wish I could have someone who would help me create the world!' He said to himself.

As he carefully crafted his wishes in his head, out sprang a lady from his mouth! She was dressed in white and looked beautiful. She also carried an Indian lute (veena). Lord Brahma was pleased with his first creation. His eyes glowed with pride. 'I shall call you Saraswati, the Goddess of speech and learning,' He told her.

The goddess thanked Brahma for creating her. She requested him, 'Lord, please be at peace and continue working with your creations while I play to you a string of soothing musical notes (ragas) on my veena that will inspire you to create further.' Henceforth, Goddess Saraswati became Lord Brahma's companion.

As Lord Brahma meditated, Goddess Saraswati started playing the veena. Her soothing music helped Brahma to get into the flow that helped his wonderful creations come to life! Mountains were created. Oceans were filled with water. Seasons were created and they changed at regular intervals, with perfection. The sun, the moon and the planets, were all created.

Looking at his creations, Lord Brahma became arrogant and greedy and thought he had done it all by himself. He did not realise that Saraswati's knowledge brought life to those creations. He thought to himself, 'I shall bring her under my control.' The goddess immediately understood Brahma's intentions. She decided to flee heaven. In his pursuit of Saraswati, Brahma followed. In whichever direction the goddess went, a head would spring out from Brahma. Brahma, now, came to have five heads!

Lord Shiva, the Lord of transformation, noticed this. He confided in Mahamaya, the Supreme Goddess, 'I need to stop Brahma from being disrespectful to the Goddess as creation cannot happen without knowledge and Saraswati is the very embodiment of wisdom.'

Shiva then, decided to cut the head of Brahma to aid Saraswati. Brahma now, had four heads and realised that knowledge was everywhere if one chose to look and that it could not be controlled. The more it was shared the more it benefitted everyone. That was the boon given by Saraswati.

Saraswati had had enough of the heavens and decided to reside on earth and bless humans with knowledge and wisdom. Any skill or knowledge that is given to us by our teachers and parents, is considered to be a blessing of Goddess Saraswati.

Sculptors and artists have been inspired by the goddess since ancient times. She is often shown with four hands with which she bestows us with a clear mind, intellect, alertness and self-confidence. In each of her hands she carries a string of crystal beads, the four Vedas and a pot of sacred water.

Saraswati also holds an Indian lute (veena) through which she teaches us to have control over our actions. She is seated on a white lotus, a symbol of light, purity and truth. She also rides a swan or a peacock which does not spread its feathers in her presence. Goddess Saraswati always inspires us to be humble in search for knowledge.

Basant Panchami is celebrated as the day of Spring when life evolves. It is also the day dedicated to Goddess Saraswati. It is said that during this time, She loves to wear clothes in yellow and decorate herself with yellow flowers. Books are also worshipped as a mark of respect for knowledge and the wisdom they offer mankind.

The importance of Goddess Saraswati remains as a symbol of the light of knowledge which sheds all darkness. It is knowledge that has helped humans to be different from the rest of the animal kingdom. It has given us wisdom and has helped us build a better world!

SARASWATI

Brahma needed to create the world but he could not do it alone. Guess who came to the rescue? The goddess of wisdom herself. In this tale of wonder, enjoy the creation and legend of Goddess Saraswati!

Om Books International

Reprinted in 2024

Corporate & Editorial Office
A-12, Sector 64, Noida 201 301,
Uttar Pradesh, India
Phone: +91 120 477 4100
Email: editorial@ombooks.com
Website: www.ombooksinternational.com

Sales Office
107, Ansari Road, Darya Ganj,
New Delhi 110 002, India
Phone: +91 11 4000 9000
Email: sales@ombooks.com
Website: www.ombooks.com

ISBN: 978-93-84119-63-8

Printed in India

10 9 8 7 6 5 4 3 2

ISBN 978-93-84119-63-8 US $ 3.99 £ 3.50

9 789384 119638

www.ombooksinternational.com

0012500

Om KIDZ

eBOOK available